MABEL LUCIE ATTWELL

MABEL
LUCIE
ATTWELL

MABEL LUCIE ATTWELL

CHRIS BEETLES

PAVILION
MICHAEL JOSEPH

To Alexander and his Grandparents

First published in Great Britain in 1988 by
PAVILION BOOKS LIMITED
196 Shaftesbury Avenue, London WC2H 8JL
in association with Michael Joseph Limited
27 Wrights Lane, Kensington, London W8 5TZ

Designed by Bridgewater Design
Illustration page 34: Robert Opie Collection

British Library Cataloguing in Publication Data

Beetles, Chris
Mabel Lucie Attwell.
1. Attwell, Mabel Lucie 2. Illustrators — England —
Biography
I. Title
741.942   NC978.5.A8

ISBN 1-85145-282-6

Printed and bound in Spain by Graficas Estella

*ILLUSTRATION ON PAGE 2 'The Bride, God Bless
her. The Bridegroom, God help him!' A Postcard
design.*

CONTENTS

MABEL LUCIE ATTWELL
– AN APPRECIATION

*OPPOSITE Mabel Lucie by her artist daughter,
Peggy Wickham.*

Every bathroom should have one, and for over fifty years most did.

PLEASE REMEMBER – DON'T FORGET! – NEVER LEAVE THE BATHROOM WET . . .

The washable bathroom plaque became the most popular image of this century's best-loved illustrator, Mabel Lucie Attwell.

NOR LEAVE THE SOAP STILL IN THE WATER – THAT'S A THING YOU NEVER OUGHT'ER! . . .

It sold in hundreds of thousands throughout half a century, because it had all the elements that made Mabel Lucie Attwell a success: simplicity of design, striking colour, charm and cute kids, but above all a message. Mabel Lucie was an illustrator who knew how to communicate. The message was classless: between the Wars all levels of society bought it and hung it in the bathroom as a jokey talisman for good behaviour. It may be a piece of bossy doggerel but it is fun and was beloved of landladies from Blackpool to Bognor, hoping to soften the edge of their regimented homeliness.

AND AS YOU'VE BEEN SO OFTEN TOLD, NEVER LET THE 'HOT' RUN 'COLD'; . . .

From Cambridge to Kensington Gore mothers purchased it in order to control the bathing excesses of all the family, a Moses tablet for middle-class ablutions. Indeed, the nanny may have recited it to her pink-skinned charge and so inculcated an even closer relationship between cleanliness and godliness, but it was essentially a message from the grown-ups to their soapy, soaking peers, an attempt to take the steam out of the family battleground.

NOR LEAVE THE TOWELS UPON THE FLOOR, NOR KEEP THE BATH AN HOUR OR MORE – WHEN OTHER FOLKS ARE WANTING ONE; JUST DON'T FORGET – IT ISN'T DONE! . . .

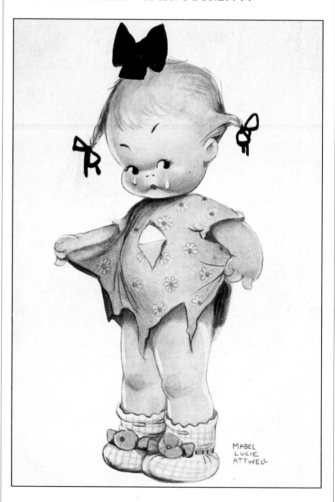

ABOVE *Mabel Lucie's toddler had her first bath in 1929. This design for a bathroom plaque became the most famous of her images.*

ABOVE *Her postcards were exported to almost every country in the world. 'Them Laundries!' when reprinted in India became 'Dem dhobies'.*

Mabel Lucie's dictums are from the mouths of babes and toddlers, but directed to the sophisticated and regulated adult world. The chubby, pink-cheeked and moon-faced little beings intoned the rhymes in all the pictures, but it was the carefully observed demeanour and posture of these cute archetypes that were the only childish components. The sentiments were for a world far less spontaneous.

AN' IF YOU'D REALLY DO THE THING –
THERE'S NOT THE SLIGHTEST NEED TO SING!

By the time the bathroom plaque appeared in 1929 Mabel Lucie Attwell was at the peak of her popularity, producing twenty-four postcard designs annually. Valentines, the publishers, reported that one design sometimes sold half a million copies a month. The postcards were exported to almost every country in the world with appropriate changes in the title to capture a local nuance: a toddler dressed in shredded clothes complains about 'Them laundries!' in the United Kingdom, but when reprinted for the British Raj in the 1930s the caption is 'Dem dhobies!'

Sustained commercial success of this size is a publishing phenomenon that is only partly explained by the universal appeal of childhood's pretty innocence. Another ingredient was touched on by Mabel Lucie in a newspaper interview later in her life: 'I am mixed up with children,' she said, 'but I draw mainly for adults: the suburbanite, the mother, the *demi-mondaine,* the country gossip, the cockney housewife, the young married couple, the shopgirl, the flapper, the faithful wife and the unfaithful, the "grown-up" and the not so good. I see the child in an adult. Then I draw the adult as a child. The situation, the stance and the vocabulary are taken from the children. But the message is between two adults – between me and any other. Children would not understand that message.'

The endearing toddlers portrayed may not have understood, but in their starring roles they give sanction to the racy caption and sweeten the saucy *double entendre*. 'An' you know what men are!' (page 29); 'Everybody's doing it'; 'What's the use of a perfect day when you can't have a perfect night?' were, for example, all well-known titles and no one was scandalized. The appeal was in sending messages that were just nicely suggestive, to which no one would dare to object. In 1962 Peter Laurie, a feature writer for *Vogue,* succinctly summed this up: 'Her cards solve a million problems of communicaton for the repressed English.'

The caption was very important to the artist: 'I

BELOW Frontispiece to The Water Babies *by Charles Kingsley, published in 1915 by Raphael Tuck and Sons.*

can't start on a drawing until I've finally decided upon the title', she told *Strand Magazine* in 1936. 'In fact I never put pencil to paper until I have found a title that satisfies me. Sometimes I'll have discarded twenty or thirty titles before I light upon the one that perfectly hits off the little notion I'm aiming at.'

This determination to get things right characterizes all her work, and the apparent simplicity of her art belies the perfectionist endeavour behind it. The best performance is usually the best rehearsed, the best ad lib, the most practised; Mabel Lucie's easy charm comes from an obsessive professionalism hidden from view. As a result, she continued to remain at the top of her field throughout her life, secure from the threat of failure.

When asked, however, what her greatest achievement was in life, she didn't point to the fame of her work, but said: 'My marriage, no, first baby. Achievement is the wrong word, but yes, motherhood was the most wonderful thing in my life. My career is me and my pictures are me, but no artist, or writer – or scientist – could make anything as perfect as a baby, and yet through me it had been done. I couldn't believe it.'

The love within her own family was certainly the inspiration for her best work and for much of her subject matter: 'All my paintings are the outcome of quaint and beautiful things I have seen at tucking-up time, or moments almost as eventful in baby life. It is then that I see deep into their little minds, and I am grateful for having the receptiveness of brain to retain the dainty secrets I have seen.' As a mother she gave her children the attention that she had craved in her own childhood.

There is no doubting where Mabel Lucie stands in her attitude to children. She pleads an emphatic 'guilty' to sentimentalization of childhood – a recurring adverse criticism of her work; but can those sneering art critics suggest a safer, healthier and more natural attitude?

Mabel Lucie was born on 4 June, 1879 in Mile End, London, the ninth of ten children of Augustus and Ann Attwell. Three children died in infancy. Her father was a butcher at Mile End and they lived in a large red-brick house called Collingwood in north-west London. There are some happy memories of the enclosing bustle of family life, its security behind the thick curtained windows and its cosiness with the coal fires and the cooking of batches of pastries and cakes and large joints in the shining black kitchen range. However, her pretty, passive mother did not seem to have provided enough affection, as the baby sister, Jess, was the parents' favourite. Jealousies and anxieties grew in Mabel Lucie (there was a fear of a tiger in the cupboard at the turn of the stairs) and a craving for love. She remembers praying in the lavatory for her mother to like her, and longing to own a doll of her own and wheel it in her own pram. All of this she was only able to express in moods (her brother teasingly called her the Tragedy Queen), infatuations, day-dreams and story-telling. These stories about families and babies led to her making little sketches to illustrate them.

Though her own abilities went partly unnoticed in the face of so much artistic and musical talent in the family (Norman became a cellist and conductor, Jess, the youngest, a brilliant concert pianist for a while, and Emily, the eldest, an accomplished water-colourist), something rather individual had started to develop. 'What is it about that child? There's something behind the eyes . . .', she overheard a visitor say to her mother and although she went at once to a looking-glass to discover what could be there, she could see nothing but her own large, blue, expressive eyes looking anxiously back at her.

Self-conscious shyness continued into her teens, when she recalls adoring silently a friend of her brother and, finding his hat in the hall one day, she quickly kissed it. The sad but affectionate girl sought refuge in her imagination, which, combined with her ability to draw, gave her some outside approval and a successful outlet for her talents. 'When I was 15, my family thought I had gone completely mad. While they were becoming brilliant musicians, I suddenly announced that I had sent two pictures to a publisher. They laughed. A few days later, I received an envelope by post. They were all watching me when I opened it. Inside was a cheque for two guineas.'

Her father was a man of unusual temperament and views, a man of rectitude, with progressive if idiosyncratic ideas. He was an agnostic, pro-Boer and a homeopathist who had sea water brought to London for his bath. Unfortunately he was a homeopathist who wouldn't let his children go to a dentist and this, coupled with a passion for Everton toffee and liberal dispensing of sweets, led to agonies of toothache for Mabel Lucie. She remembers him, however, with love, admiration and respect for he was a just and sensitive father in his Victorian way. He is remembered as having always being an 'elderly' man with his handsome, pink bald head fringed with white hair and a drooping white moustache. 'My father was a man of great integrity . . . and he said that whatever we did we must learn to do for ourselves. I played the piano. My mother used to sigh, "Oh, please, not now Mab", as soon as I opened the lid of the piano. My father who was a perfectionist would say patiently, "It isn't right Mab." I inherited that streak of perfectionism. Sometimes I have been forced to end a contract because I must have my pictures perfect.'

'I was never any good at lessons because I was most of the time scribbling pictures of chldren all over my exercise books. After my schooldays were over, I thought I might be able to sell some of my drawings for pocket money. I shall never forget the day when I went in fear and trembling to a publisher's office near Leicester Square – nor can I forget how I felt when I came home with a cheque for a whole guinea in my pocket!

'Soon after that I was doing quite a lot of work for

ABOVE 'Christmas Eve'. A 1911 frontispiece to
Little Folks. *Strong design and flat blocks of
colour show the London Sketch Club's influence.*

been the main influences on her during those years.
What had happened to make her produce, by 1910,
an illustration so mature, accomplished and satis-
fying as the one in the Christmas edition of *Little
Folks?*

St Martin's School of Art had given her a patchy
but basic grounding, but more importantly it had
given Mabel Lucie her future husband. There she
had met and fallen in love with Harold Earnshaw, a
gifted draughtsman in pen, ink and watercolour. He
was 'a slim, fair-haired, blue-eyed young man who
had been a choir boy and had a pleasant light tenor
voice'. His jaunty, optimistic manner and affection
for her provided the security and love with which
she could reverse the unhappiness of childhood, and
his sociability offered her the artistic milieu in
which her art was to develop.

They married in 1908, taking a bus to the
registry office. There was no one from the family
present, but happily there happened to be a
barrel organ outside and they left to the tune of
'When we are married'. Mabel Lucie may have felt
at the time that it was a determined bid for indepen-
dence from her family background, an escape from
pecking order domesticity. As both Harold and she
had commissions to illustrate books, the future felt
assured as they went off to honeymoon in Babba-
combe Bay in Devon. 'We found we had £50 each,
and that seemed a great deal of money, and quite
enough to get married on. So we did, and took a
cottage in Devon for the summer. He had his book to
do, and I had mine. We weren't married long but we
were happy.'

They lived in a flat in Dulwich at first and it was
there that Peggy, their daughter, was born in 1909.
The birth was long and difficult and, when sum-
moned, the woman doctor was heard to say, 'Oh good
– my first patient.' So was born not only Mr and
Mrs Earnshaw's little girl, but also the original and
definitive Mabel Lucie Attwell toddler. Some
features of the infants in the W. & R. Chambers'
books and in the jolly originals done for *Little Folks*
magazine are the antecedents of characters in the
generation of postcard kids to come. However it is
Peggy in the first years of the War who is obviously
the Attwell model. Family photographs of this extra-
ordinarily pretty child (page 10) need only be briefly
compared with the early postcard designs to prove
this point.

Artists, and particularly illustrators, are more ef-
fective when they put something of their own experience into a picture. 'Drawn from memory' becomes
accuracy modified by personality and a romantic dis-

publishers. Not important, but it was enough to live
on and to pay my fees at the art schools where I
studied for five hard years. So, you see, practically
from the time I left school I've been able to earn my
bread and butter as an artist.'

Her years, first at Heatherleys, a private art
school, and then at St Martin's School of Art were
uncongenial and her attendance was desultory, with
little enthusiasm for classical drawing. She was glad
to leave and take up a series of commissions from
the book publishers, W. & R. Chambers, to illustrate
a series of typically low-key stories by May Baldwin,
Mrs Molesworth and others. Between the first, *That
Little Limb,* in 1905 and *The February Boys* in 1909
there is a noticeable improvement: the pictures become more robust and stylish, and, as ever, what she
lacked in great draughtsmanship she made up for by
strong, clear design and the ability to communicate
the delights of a fantasy world.

It is interesting to consider now what might have

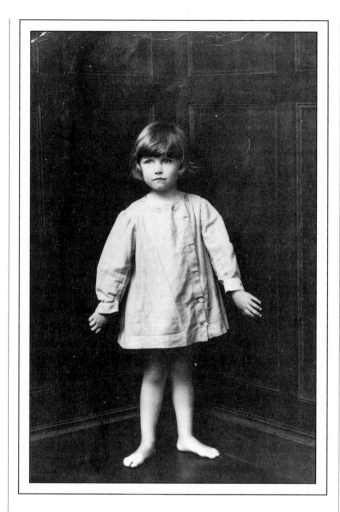

ABOVE *Daughter Peggy from the family album. Pretty, chubby cheeked and podgy kneed, she is the inspiration for the Mabel Lucie toddler.*

ABOVE *'Time for bed'. Peggy is obviously the model for this postcard child published around the time of the First World War.*

position. The imaginative story or picture that results is then that much more expressive, and produces words and images that will have a shared reality between author and reader. Mabel Lucie Attwell's art is drawn directly from her narrow but closely observed experience of life and never strays beyond what it knows. It is from her own class and from her own time and is presented with the entertaining skill of a good illustrator. Motherhood continued to be the inspirational strength of her life and career: 'Personally I consider the home and the upbringing of children the most important things in the world and for that reason I should not recommend every woman – especially those who have not any specialized talent – to combine the career of running a home with an outside business.' Today Mabel Lucie Attwell would read both the *Daily Telegraph* and the *Guardian*.

In 1908 her clubbable husband 'Pat', as H.C.

Earnshaw was always known, joined the London Sketch Club. Here was a group of mainly young, talented artists and illustrators who would meet once a week in the Wells Street Studio, London, do a two-hour sketch to an agreed theme and then mingle and chat over the Sketch Club 'hot' supper. Later there followed high-spirited renditions and entertainments by club members. It was a time of great cross-fertilization, for among the members were the brothers Charles and William Heath Robinson, John Hassall, Cecil Aldin, H. M. Bateman, Tom Browne, Harry Rountree, Lawson Wood, G. S. Studdy, Dudley Hardy, and, most significantly, James Pryde and William Nicholson. These last two, as the Beggarstaff Brothers, had influenced a change in the look of book illustration and poster advertising from the 1890s onward. Strongly outlined design, of an almost Japanese two-dimensional simplicity, brought a new impact to the visual world.

The shape of objects became more emphatic with confident black outlines enclosing flat blocks of colour. In the early 1900s Cecil Aldin did the famous Colman's Mustards advertisements, John Hassall's poster 'Skegness Is So Bracing' appeared and Tom Browne's 'Ah, Bisto' was to become part of advertising legend.

Though the London Sketch Club had a 'men only' rule the Earnshaws mixed with the artists socially and Harry Rountree in particular was a good friend of Pat with whom he played golf regularly. An article in *Strand Magazine* records the influence of Sketch Club members on Mabel Lucie Attwell: 'She showed me a number of 'two-hour' sketches by Mr Earnshaw – correct and full in every detail – made at the London Sketch Club, and hung around the studio with others executed by distinguished friends and fellow students. It is evident that she greatly admires them but says that such technical excellence was not for her.' While she would never emulate the graphic facility of those artists, her design sense was developing on parallel lines and was to equal the best. Cassell & Co.'s *Little Folks* magazine and W. & R. Chambers' book illustrations show it to a degree, but it is in the world of posters and postcards that her particular abilities matured.

Commercial firms quickly discovered that Mabel Lucie had brand appeal and the motif of childish wide-eyed wonderment and innocence was introduced into soft-sell advertising. By March 1914, an article in *Advertising World* had already recorded successful promotions for: Jaeger Footwear ('For Tiny Toes'), Swan Fountain Pens ('A Present For Daddy'), Vim ('Come and Help Mother'), and Velvet Skin Soap ('Baby Chooses' – as reported in *Nursery News)*. Best known among this work was the series she did for the London Underground, and among these 'Hullo, Did you come by Underground?' (page 34) became famous in its day, causing an exhaustive and unprecedented run on stocks of posters for sale.

Despite the busy artistic socializing in London, the young married couple were house-hunting. They would take a train to the nearest edge of suburbia and start walking. One day they saw a 'To let' board outside a little house called 'Casita' on the edge of Farthing Downs, south of Coulsdon, and both wanted it immediately. There was just enough room for them, Peggy the baby, and Nanny Simpson. It was blissfully on the edge of virgin chalk downland with fields, farms and woods stretching away. A small golf course of nine holes was conveniently near and Pat could take the train up to London for his weekly Sketch Club meeting. After the birth of

their first son, Peter (Max), in 1911 they moved to a much larger house nearby, 'Fairdene', and knocked a connecting wall down on the first floor between two bedrooms to make one large studio.

In 1910 Mabel Lucie had decided to approach the agent who looked after the careers of many successful London Sketch Club artists. Her daughter, Peggy Wickham, describes the event: '. . . trembling with nervousness, she went to visit the artists' agent Francis and Mills, whose label, bearing a picture of a medieval character in a tall crowned hat by John Hassall, announced that they were "Agents to the Best Artists". Mr Francis turned out to be a bluff man with a good business sense and a great zest for life, and as "Frankie", he became a support and friend. On her first visit he told her, "I am not interested in the work of young ladies. But leave the sketches here and I shall have a look at them." When she returned later it was to hear that he had sold them all and would be glad to have some more.

BELOW Happy days in the twenties at Little House, Rye. Left to right: husband 'Pat' Earnshaw, Peggy, Brian, known as 'Bill', and Mabel Lucie.

From that moment her work was always in demand.' Francis and Mills, now handling her work, brought in commissions for posters, advertisements and books, coloured double-spread pages in glossy magazines such as the *Tatler,* the *Bystander,* the *Graphic,* and the *Illustrated London News* and, of course, much work for women's magazines.

She now began her long association with Valentine and Sons of Dundee for whom she designed postcards, calendars, greetings

ABOVE *From 1911, Valentine & Sons of Dundee produced many millions of her postcards and ephemera. This association lasted until her death.*

Andersen's Fairy Tales in 1914, *The Water-Babies* in 1915, and *Children's Stories from French Fairy Tales* in 1917. They were produced as inexpensive colour-illustrated 'gift' books for children. The books had hard covers, twelve colour plates and many black-and-white line drawings among the abridged texts. Mab had missed illustrating the luxury colourplate volumes of the pre-War era. These were really aimed at an adult market and had been dominated by artists such as Arthur

cards, booklets, shopping lists, plaques and jigsaw puzzles until the end of her working life. An anecdote from Valentines' house journal shows her international appeal: 'Prints of her watercolour drawings taken from the *Tatler* found their way to the battle area and in this instance, decorated the walls of a certain dug-out. In the course of hostilities the dug-out was captured by the Germans who held it for eighteen months. When it was recaptured, the Attwell prints were still on the walls and had obviously been treated with great care!'

The appeal of the postcards contributed to the War effort not only through general morale boosting, but directly through recruitment and social propaganda: a tiny tot, with daddy's military hat and swagger stick points to the moon with a peremptory 'Put out that Light'; a tearful toddler points to a recruitment poster which states, 'Your King and Country Need 100,000 Men' and sadly asks, 'Why wasn't I born a Man?' – not quite the imperative power of Alfred Leetes' Kitchener poster, but tugging just as hard at the heart strings. Pat Earnshaw made up his mind in 1915 and joined up in The Artists Rifles. A year later he was dreadfully wounded and lost his right arm.

During the decade of the First World War, Mab, as Pat called her, produced some of her best-known work in illustrating fairy-tale classics first for Cassel & Co. (*Grimms' Fairy Tales*) then for Raphael Tuck & Son. It started with *Mother Goose* in 1910, *Alice in Wonderland* in 1911, followed by *Hans*

Rackham, Edmund Dulac and Warwick Goble, whereas Mabel Lucie's illustrations were for the children themselves. Hers was an accessible world of makebelieve, of fairy-tale fantasy and imagination, and children's young minds easily shared her vision and were thrilled by it. At the insistence of Sir J. M. Barrie himself Hodder & Stoughton approached Mabel Lucie to illustrate a gift-book edition of *Peter Pan and Wendy* which appeared in 1921. It became a bestseller, and rightly so, as it was to be thumbed to loving death in nurseries, generation after generation. In her role as an illustrator for children it is the most successful of her books, as it touches most enjoyably on the areas of that marvellous story in a way that children can understand and remember forever. Mabel Lucie's *Peter Pan and Wendy* has been compared unfavourably with Arthur Rackham's *Peter Pan in Kensington Gardens* published in 1906. Rackham, without doubt one of the greatest illustrators of fiction, produced a very special group of pictures but to compare them with Mabel Lucie's is pointless since the appeal of each is totally different.

Fame increased throughout the twenties, a decade that had started for Mabel Lucie with both Pathe Pictorial and Gaumont Gazette, the rival cinema newsreels, showing separate interviews with her in the same week. In 1922 Cyril Gamon, a publisher, came to see her at Fairdene to ask her to produce a Lucie Attwell annual. It was published at first by S. W. Partridge & Co. and then by Dean & Son and continued uninterrupted from 1922 until 1974 (it

"WHY
WASN'T
I BORN
A MAN?"

MABEL
LUCIE
ATTWELL

ABOVE This First World War postcard helped recruitment with its strong emotional appeal. BELOW RIGHT 'I won't go to bed' from Peter Pan and Wendy *by J. M. Barrie. It's bedtime for Michael at the insistence of Nana the nurse.*

The world of makebelieve was still very vivid in 1922 when Mabel Lucie had an intrepid and exciting adventure of her own. Having established a working relationship with Marie, the Queen of Roumania, three years earlier with the collaborative publication of *Peeping Pansy* published by Hodder and Stoughton, Mabel Lucie was invited to stay with her royal admirer in Bucharest with a view to producing more work together. This was her first time abroad, and the whole trip was to prove quite an extraordinary experience, giving her a wonderful insight into a very different culture. In a letter home she revealed how strongly she felt the difference: 'Poor shy little me, pitched right into the very middle of a Royal family. Ceremony and trappings complete.'

These two remarkable women had an immediate affinity for one another and Mabel Lucie found her hostess, 'a charming and delightful woman [who] looks topping in the Roumanian costume which she wears'. The Queen held a mutual respect for Mabel Lucie and the work she produced. Both women had a deep love of children and the world in which they grew up, and Mabel Lucie's particular approach in depicting them greatly appealed to the Queen. She confided to Mabel Lucie that she kept her books near her, 'as comfort for when I am in the dumps.'

Mabel Lucie was much inspired by what she saw, not only in Roumania, but throughout Europe on the four week journey to the Royal Palace. She travelled with Alan Francis, her first publishing ally, known to all as 'Frankie', visiting as many towns and cities as possible. The images used after her trip vary enormously and show a much wider range of influences.

was continued after her death in 1964 with the re-use of past material). She drew all of each annual herself: the colour cover, black-and-white drawings and some colour pages, and wrote many of the stories and verses. She still found time in the early twenties to invent a new type of fairy for Valentine & Sons. Called a Boo Boo it was a merry cross between an elfin-like pisky and a leprechaunlette dressed in Lincoln Green. Anyway the Boo Boos lived happily with Bunty in a series of successful booklets between 1921–22. They went on to materialize into the third dimension in the form of Boo Boo soft toys, and made many public appearances in various other forms such as nursery tea services. In recent years they have even come back from the dead (but only just) as Boo Boo dolls.

'Children blue eyed and flaxen haired' whom she saw in Altdorf in Switzerland seem to have created the short story character of the Princess in *The Princess and the Bird of Ill Omen* (page 62). *Nicu, the Smiler* (page 66), who appears in the Lucie Attwell Annual of 1925 wears a costume definitely inspired by the 'picturesque peasants' with whom she was so impressed in Roumania. No longer then is the main model her own daughter, Peggy, as in *Peeping Pansy,* and The Boo-Boo Books of 1919 and 1921–22 respectively.

Her Roumanian adventure ended on 13 July 1922. Although homesick and missing her husband and babies, Mabel Lucie declared it, 'A delightful wondrous visit'.

Merchandising of the Attwell image continued throughout the thirties and forties. Good-quality china figures were made by Shelley pottery, and rubber dolls modelled from Plasticine images by Mabel Lucie (often with fashionable accoutrements) appeared with names like 'Snookums', 'Girlie', 'Mabel Lucie', 'The Toddler', 'Little Happy' and, the star of them all, 'Diddums' whose demise was even mentioned with sadness in the first line of Mabel Lucie's *Times* obituary.

Perhaps the happiest days of the Earnshaw family were in the late twenties, when, after many moves,

ABOVE *From* The Boo-Boos and Bunty's Baby, *1920.*

they settled in Cranley Gardens, London. As Peggy Wickham put it, '. . . they moved to a large, tall house in South Kensington where the prosperous and gay years began . . . they were both doing well with their work, domestic staff were obtainable, the children at school or art school and, with a circle of friends, they enjoyed dances, *thé dansants,* balls, dinners at the Mansion House, films, clubs and theatres. Mabel Lucie had her hair shingled, she read and talked a lot, and Pat had his billiards and golf and the Chelsea Arts Club. They bought their first car, a top-heavy Buick, and enjoyed outings to the country.

In the summer holidays, they rented rooms for the family in a Sussex farmhouse (Church Farm, Littlington) and became so attached to the Cuckmere Valley near Alfriston that they decided to look for a house there. They sold the London house after their daughter's marriage in 1930 and bought Manor Farmhouse, West Dean, Sussex.

Then the dancing had to stop: Pat's health began to fail and the younger son, Bill, died unexpectedly of pneumonia at the age of twenty. With the family dispersed, her husband ill, and unwell herself from grief,

Mabel Lucie decided to leave the country house and go back to London, where Pat died in 1936 after a prolonged illness. She was by now doing fewer posters and advertisements, but still producing her twenty-four new postcards every year, calendars, greetings cards, children's handkerchiefs, nursery china and dolls. Yet she remained a perfectionist. Once, when there was an exhibition of her dolls produced by Chad Valley Toy Company in the Christmas display at Harrods, she sent along her maid to the toy department to rearrange and cut their hair styles.'

Royal patronage came in 1937: Princess Margaret ordered her personalized Christmas card 'There are Fairies (page 60), and the following year 'Christmas Eve'; Mabel Lucie Attwell china was used in the nurseries of Princesses Elizabeth and Margaret; and Prince Charles owned a set of nursery china, a gift from the Queen in 1949. This shows once more Mabel Lucie Attwell's continuity of appeal from generation to generation.

During the Second World War, after bomb damage to both her London properties, she moved to Froxfield, Wiltshire, expecting the demand for her work to fall off. This did not happen, but she was receiving less publicity now and was becoming less fashionable. She was never short of work and in 1943 she additionally started the black-and-white strip cartoon for *London Opinion* called 'Wot a Life'. She moved to Fowey in Cornwall in 1945 with her

ABOVE The original designs for the famous Diddums rubber doll made by the Chad Valley Toy Company.
RIGHT Pat and Mabel Lucie stepping out in the gay and prosperous years of the late 1920s.
BELOW Mabel Lucie's ephemera came in all shapes and sizes and with a multitude of uses. Her 'Fairy Tree' served as a money box as well as a biscuit tin.

son Peter and stayed there for the last twenty years of her life, with Valentines keeping her busy on the Lucie Attwell Annuals.

The occasional reporter rediscovered her. Peter Laurie was surprised in 1962 to find his prejudices overturned: 'An old woman of character is the refined *prima materia* of humanity: the vanities of twenty, the dignities of forty, the regrets of sixty have all burned away; only the real human is left. This is what she is; someone worth remembering.'

Peggy Wickham, her daughter, became a talented artist and illustrator and helped her with some of her later work. Much of the information in this book is based on her reminiscences and she best sums up her mother's life and her last days: 'She had more than the usual number of difficulties to

face and some tragedies during her life, which spanned two World Wars, but although a rather anxious person with an "artistic temperament" and great sensitivity, she had tremendous vitality, courage and drive. Her work was what she wanted to be doing and she was indomitable. "What a personality! There was no one like her!" one of her publishers said, and meant it.

'She died peacefully on 5 November 1964. It had been an exceptionally still, mellow day and as she lay with her eyes shut, the pink evening light of sunset came over the water and boats and the little houses of Polruan outside her window. As evening faded, the bangs and traceries, and lights of rockets and fireworks began, for it was Guy Fawkes night. "I have had a lively life", she had said to her daughter not long before she died.'

BIOGRAPHICAL SUMMARY

Mabel Lucie's daughter, Peggy – the architypal Attwell child.

1879

Born 4 June, Mile End, London

1894

Sells first illustration

1895-1900

Attends Heatherleys and St Martin's School of Art

1905-1913

Illustrates 10 books for W. & R. Chambers

1906

Designs poster for London Underground, 'Hullo, Did you come by Underground?'

1908

Marries Harold Earnshaw

1909

Daughter Peggy born, Dulwich, London
Moves to first house, 'Casita', Coulsdon, Surrey

1910

Joins artists' agent, Francis & Mills
Mother Goose, first of the 'gift books' for Raphael Tuck and Sons

1911

Son Peter (Max) born, Coulsdon
First postcards for Valentine & Sons
Alice in Wonderland published

1914

Son Brian (Bill) born, Coulsdon

1915

Harold joins The Artists Rifles
The Water Babies for Raphael Tuck and Sons

1916

Harold wounded in France, loses right arm

1919

Peeping Pansy by Marie, Queen of Roumania, for Hodder & Stoughton

1920

The Boo-Boos are born

1922

Visit to Queen Marie in Bucharest, Roumania
First of the Lucie Attwell Annuals

1924

The Lost Princess by Marie, Queen of Roumania, for Hodder and Stoughton

1926

Move to house in South Kensington

1927

Bathroom plaque, 'Please Remember, Don't Forget'

1930

Daughter marries, becomes Peggy Wickham

1932

Moves to Manor House, West Dean, Sussex

1934

Son Bill dies, aged 20

1935

Moves back to London (Cambridge Place) to nurse Pat

1936

Pat dies

1937

Moves to 2 Ladbroke Terrace, London
Princess Margaret chooses 'There are Fairies' as her Christmas card

1940

Moves to Froxfield, Wiltshire

1941

Death of her father, aged 93 years

1945

Moves to Fowey, Cornwall

1964

Dies, 5 November, aged 85

THE ILLUSTRATIONS

OPPOSITE 'Ponk!' First used as a postcard and later adapted in cut out form as a calender. The ultimate rounded, cuddly and sentimental Mabel Lucie image.

'Come away down'. An early image almost certainly
inspired by The Water Babies of 1915. Pretty, naturalistic,
in a limited colour range, it is characteristic of work
around the War years.

OPPOSITE 'I know,' said Philippa quietly. 'I did
think of that, and of course it would break my
heart for you to go.' From The Old Pincushion by
Mrs Molesworth of 1910. This early book
illustration appeared before Mabel Lucie had
created her own stylistic images and shows the
influence of Art Nouveau in the decorative border.

CHRISTMAS."

PREVIOUS PAGES 'To Wish you a Happy Christmas'. One of the earliest postcard designs. The child's face is closer to those in the pre-1910 book illustrators rather than the Mabel Lucie archetype.

OPPOSITE 'Mary Maud Marigold Madeline Marty'. Mabel Lucie's talents extended to writing her own verses and captions throughout her working life. This early image is a rare insight into an adult world and one of which her London Sketch Club friends would have approved.

Our Mary Maud Marigold Madeline Marty,
Had such a nice invite — to such a nice party.
But (isn't it sad?) — the child's in despair,
Like Flora McFlimsy — she'd nothing to wear.
    "I know!" said our Poll — when
        she'd thought for a while —
    "I'll jolly well go in a wreath
        and a smile —!"

MABEL
LUCIE
ATTWELL

*'I hope they're not referring to me'. Always topical,
her postcards were about the concerns of the adult
world: here, the post-War imbalance of the sexes.*

'An' you know what men are!' The endearing
toddlers portrayed may not have understood, but
in their starring roles they give sanction to the
racy caption and sweeten the saucy double
entendre.

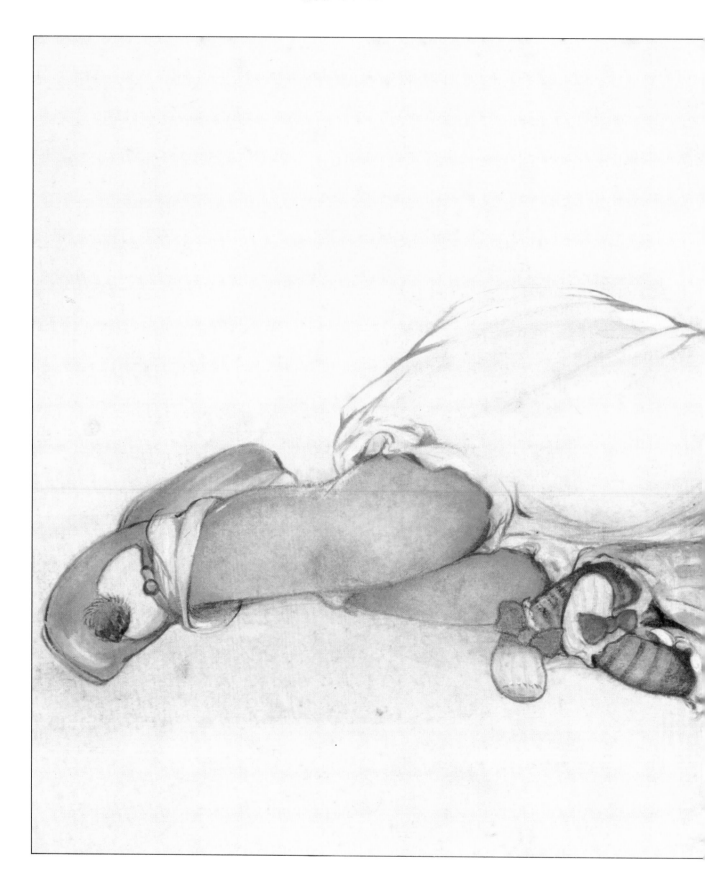

MABEL
LUCIE
ATTWELL

PREVIOUS PAGES 'The Broken Doll'. *The postcard designs started with much detail and natural complex tones. This and the recognizable, simple emotions of childhood emerge from a Victorian tradition.*
OPPOSITE *The naughty mischievous child full of tears and remorse after being punished and put in the corner has again borrowed its content from nineteenth-century art. The model is more updated.*

MABEL
LUCIE
ATTWELL

A clear, bold design for a brochure cover.

OPPOSITE 'Hullo! Did you come by
Underground?' This advertising poster was the
best known of the series she did for the London
Underground in the pre-First World War years.

Hullo! Did you come by Underground?

DISTRICT RAILWAY PLEASURE RESORTS

SPECIAL THROUGH CARS AND
CHEAP FARES FOR PARTIES OF
50 OR MORE FROM ANY STATION
TO WHICH DISTRICT TRAINS RUN.

FOR PARTICULARS,
RATES, ETC.
APPLY
ELECTRIC RAILWAY HOUSE,
BROADWAY, WESTMINSTER, SW.

TO SOUTH HARROW
EASTCOTE OR
RUISLIP.

During 1914

War Shortage! — Mauvers' Got No Back
Curtains Now!

MABEL
LUCIE
ATTWELL

PREVIOUS PAGES *'Mother's been to the Sales!'*
Fashion conscious Mabel Lucie introduced a joke
about 1914–18 austerity. The idea is developed
further with an alternative title, 'Mother's got no
bedroom curtains now!'
OPPOSITE *'A Little Bit of Fluff'. The appeal is*
irresistible: this illustration for the annual,
Printer's Pie, *shows sophisticated fashion of the*
most risqué type in 1916 – but the clothes are put
on a cute child and suddenly all is innocence and
acceptable.

PREVIOUS PAGES 'Where do flies go in the Wintertime?' One of the best of her postcard designs, this has spare graphic line and good rhythm. It also combines good narrative humour with a send-up of the old metaphysical joke. OPPOSITE 'Just look at me – Fido.' The commercial appeal of the postcards was often doubled with the affectionate bonding between the ubiquitous Mabel Lucie dog and its sweet owner. In this relationship the dog always had the upper hand.

'They are the children who fall out of their perambulators.' From Peter Pan and Wendy.

OPPOSITE *'Peter kept watch'. From* Peter Pan and Wendy *by J. M. Barrie, published by Hodder and Stoughton in 1921. The celebrated author chose Mabel Lucie to illustrate his bestseller. It was to be thumbed to loving death in nurseries, generation after generation.*

'"They don't want us to land," he explained.' The intrepid boy, Peter Pan, who never wants to grow up, brings the Darling family children to the Neverland. Mabel Lucie fans will recognize the starry-eyed fairies from previous illustrated books.

'I daresay it will hurt a little.' A world of adult
responsibilities and domesticity, peopled by
children, was a notion that would come easily to
Mabel Lucie, an experienced postcard artist.

PREVIOUS PAGES 'Starkey sighted Nibs
disappearing through the woods.' The Lost Boys of
the Neverland always live in dread of Captain
Hook and his pirates. Mabel Lucie's pirates keep
the fear at an acceptable level for children.
OPPOSITE 'When Wendy grew up'. It was planned
for Wendy to return once a year to the Neverland to
do Peter Pan's spring cleaning. It is as well the
arrangement didn't last, for the illustrator was
also rooted in the fantasy world of childhood.

*PREVIOUS PAGES 'The Broken Wing'. One of the
first postcard designs, it has an appealing fairy
lightness added to a fashionably bobbed Attwell
baby. The birds on the stylized branch have all the
comic rapport of a Thelwell sparrow.*
OPPOSITE 'My,' said Willie, 'What a lot there are!'
The Mushroom Men *from* The Lucie Attwell
Annual *published by S. W. Partridge & Co. from
1922–26. It then changed its name to* Lucie
Attwell's Children's Book *from 1927–32. Dean &
Son took over publication in 1933 and changed the
title again to* Lucie Attwell's Annual *which ran
until 1974. This image is from her first annual of
1922.*

HAVE YOU EVER SEEN
THE MUSHROOM MEN?

The front cover of The Boo-Boos and Bunty's
Baby, *1920.*

Frontispiece for The Boo-Boos and Bunty's Baby.

'What are you and what do you want?' From The
Boo-Boos and Bunty's Baby.

'They simply made themselves so small (Boo-
Boos, can you remember?) that they all fitted into
one bed.' From The Boo-Boos and Bunty's Baby.

OPPOSITE *'There are Fairies!' Although this was illustrated in* Lucie Attwell's Children's Book *as early as 1926, it brought royal patronage to Mabel Lucie in 1937 as a personalized Christmas card for Princess Margaret.*

'She looked fearlessly into the bird's cruel eyes'.
From The Princess and the Bird of Ill-Omen *by
Marie, Queen of Roumania in* Lucie Attwell's
Annual, *1924.*

'They guarded him right through the night.' From the
story, Wee Willi Winkie. The artist made her illustrations
work hard for her, often re-using them in appropriate
situations several years apart. This image was firstly
shown in the 1924 Lucie Attwell Annual and then
reappeared in 1930 with the new, but wholly appropriate
title of 'Rock a bye Baby'.

PREVIOUS PAGES: LEFT 'Smiled for all they were
worth'. From Nicu the Smiler, by Marie, Queen of
Roumania, for the Lucie Attwell Annual. RIGHT
'Oh Golly, how I love you.' A postcard design from
an age of innocence when children were allowed to
love their dolls whatever the overtones.
OPPOSITE 'I don't like to be caught by him all alone
in the forest' from Peeping Pansy of 1919 by
Marie, Queen of Roumania. This illustration is as
close to Rackham and as scary as Mabel Lucie
could manage . . . Even so, the North Wind has a
benign twinkle that will stop short of real threat to
the innocent.

'You never finks of all this, when you finks of
getting wed.' The comic side of responsible
fatherhood is once more shown by the child
demonstrating the adult role. As Mabel Lucie
said, 'I see the child in an adult. Then I draw the
adult as a child.'

OPPOSITE Attwell toddlers also lent themselves
well to the comic parodies of middle-class sports
endeavour.

"HAPPY BIRTHDAY — GLADSOME MORN —
IT'S A JOLLY GOOD THING US ALL WAS BORN!"

*A greetings card design in her later, more
simplified style. The verse is as optimistic as ever.*

OPPOSITE *'Looking for the Summertime'. Over the
years the Attwell child gradually becomes more
conical and the message is as English as ever.*

'To all smokers.' The bossy message, so much more
acceptable from a child, making sensible adult
noises.

'What's good about each day of the year
You never knows what nice thing you'll hear'
In later years the fine draughtsmanship
diminishes but the use of colour is as bold,
adventurous and appropriate as ever.

PREVIOUS PAGES *After the birth of the Boo-Boos in 1920, most of Mabel Lucie's fairies were based on these model sprites. Like her babies, however, they grew in chubby-faced curiosity.*
OPPOSITE *Mabel Lucie's attitude to childhood is sentimental – she has been criticized for this, but is there a healthier, more natural approach?*

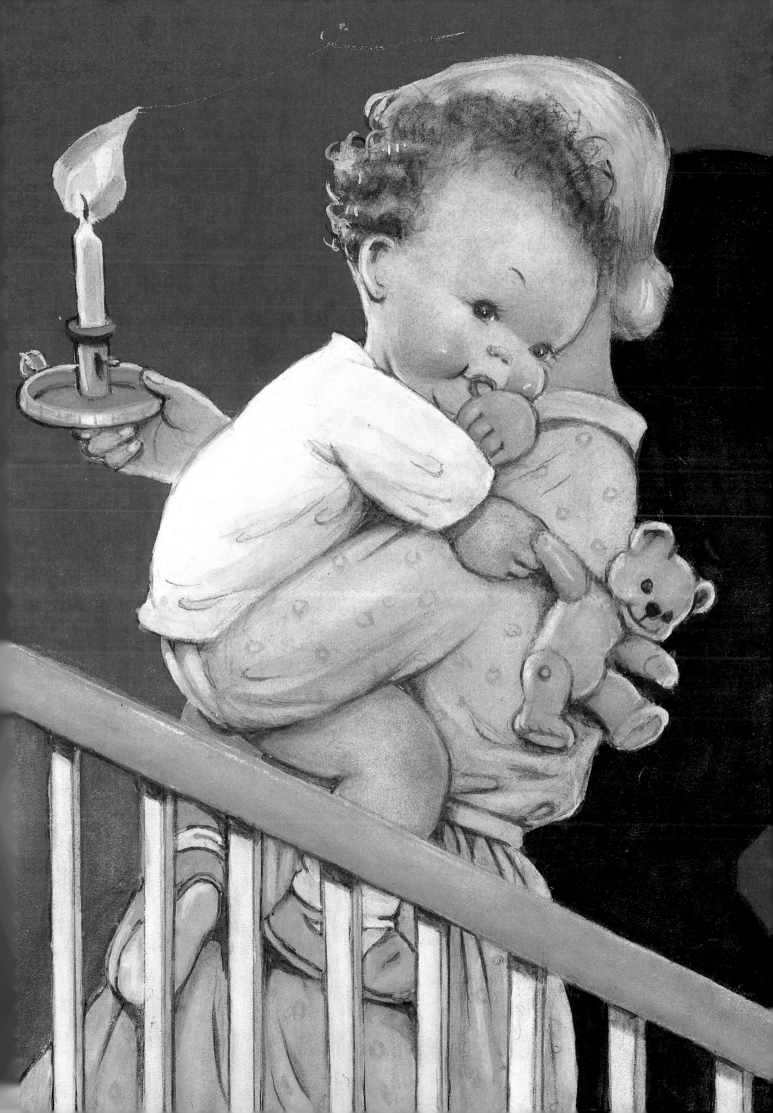

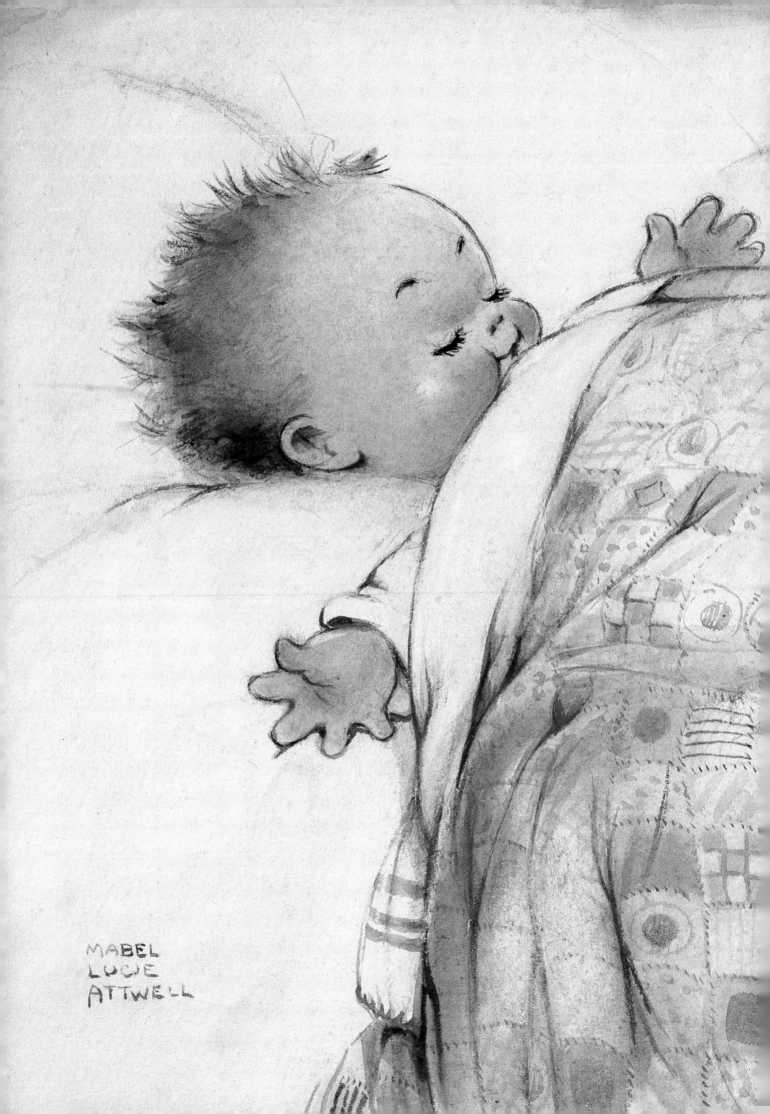

MABEL
LUCIE
ATTWELL

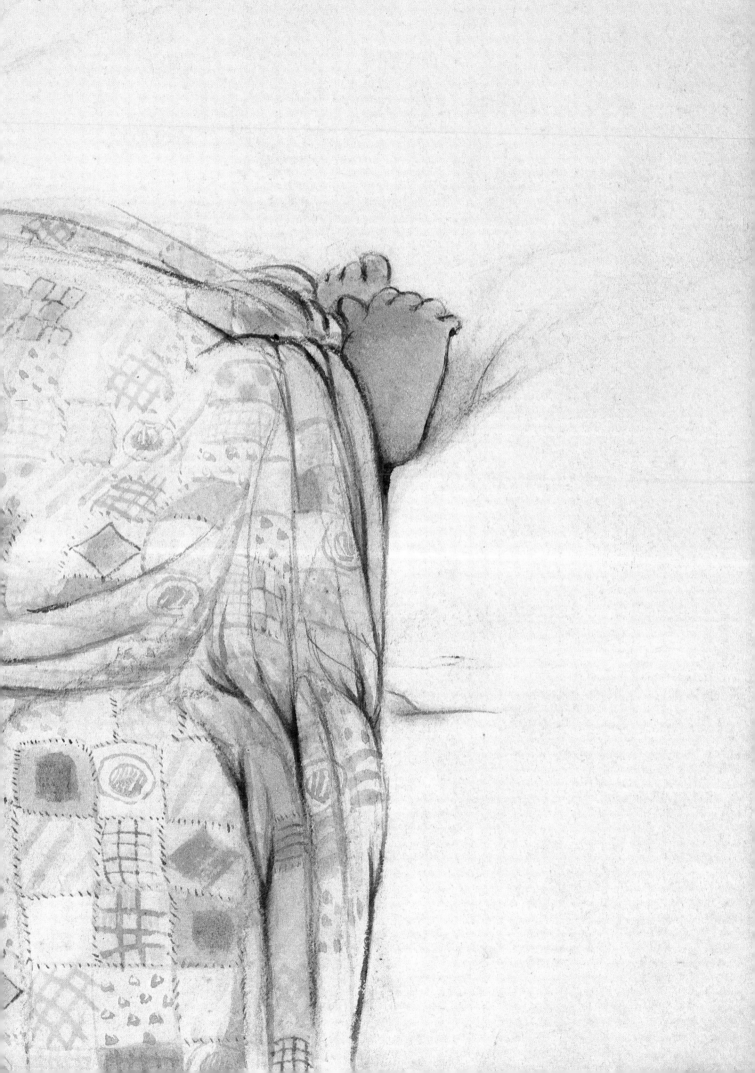

PREVIOUS PAGES
'Pleasant Dreams – sweet repose
All the bed – and all the clos!'
OPPOSITE 'If Winter comes!' Writing the caption
was the starting point for the artist. 'Sometimes
I'll have discarded twenty or thirty titles before I
light upon the one that perfectly hits off the little
notion I'm aiming at.'

MABEL
LUCIE
ATTWELL

'Sure you's swell'.

OPPOSITE *'Smiling even through the tears'. Many
of the later postcard designs are close-ups of the
toddlers' faces. But the concentrated viewpoint lies
more in observing the sentiment than underlining
the detail.*

MABEL
LUCIE
ATTWELL

PREVIOUS PAGES *'It's all lonely all alone'.*
OPPOSITE *A tearful tot. Despite being the ninth of ten children, Mabel Lucie herself recalled many unhappy and lonely moments in her childhood when she felt different from her siblings and excluded from her parents' affection.*

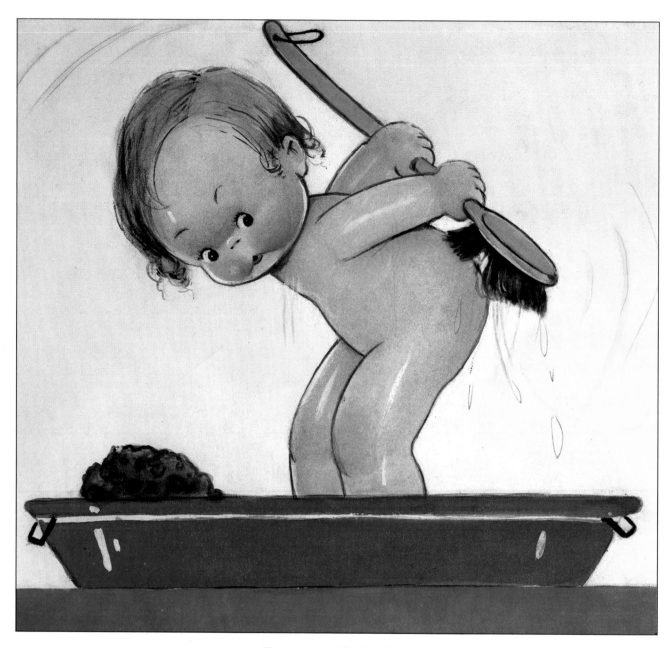

'Tomorrow will be Sunday!'

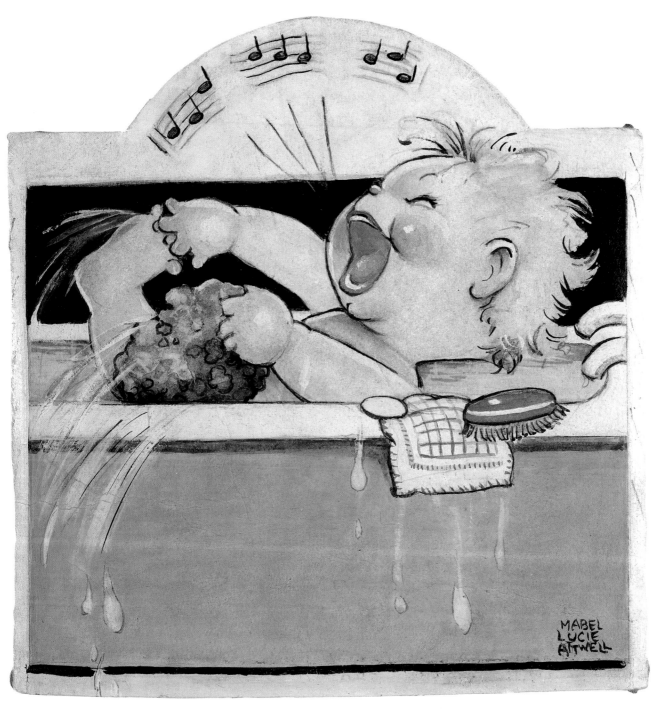

'Tra-la-la – happy morn – wot a good thing us all was
born!'

PREVIOUS PAGES 'You's the one for me!'
OPPOSITE *The experiences of motherhood gave
Mabel Lucie a direct insight into the joys of
childish games. Sometimes the enjoyment of play
is given a direct reference to the world of grown-
ups.*

'I'll try anything once!'

OPPOSITE 'As good as his mother ever made!' A
racy caption, supposedly from the mouths of
endearing tots, became acceptable. It has been said
that, 'Her cards solve a million problems of
communication for the repressed English.'

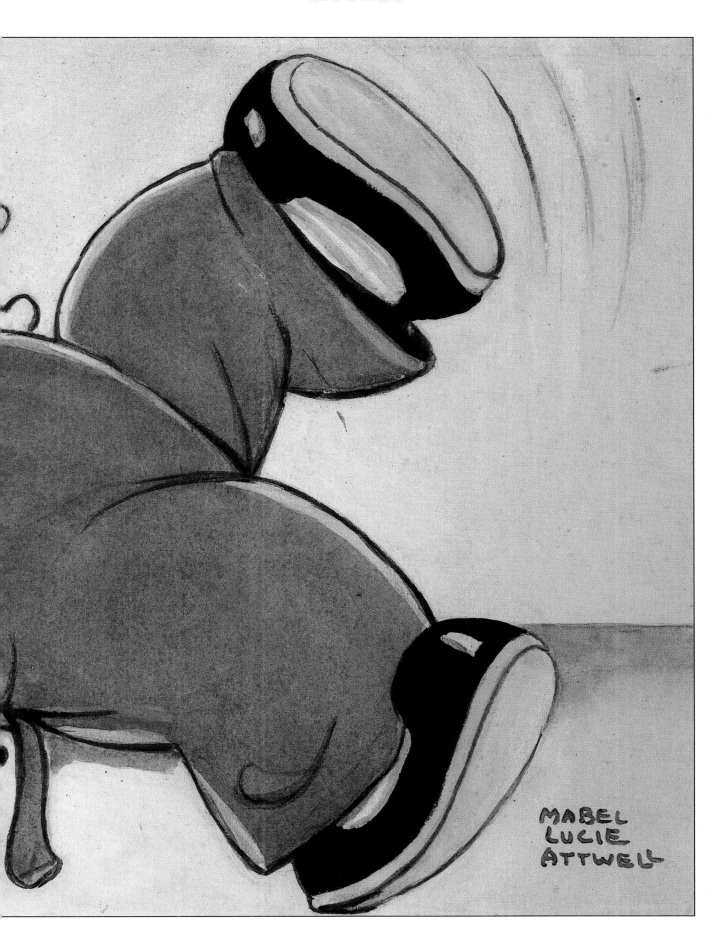

MABEL
LUCIE
ATTWELL

PREVIOUS PAGE 'Larf I must – if I bust!'
OPPOSITE 'U.R. "A.1." – U.R.!' Her postcard career
was long and prolific. Twenty-four designs each
year for more than half a century, selling millions
to every country in the world. Mabel Lucie's own
comment on her subject matter was, 'The
situation, the stance, and the vocabulary are taken
from the children. But the message is between two
adults.'

OPPOSITE *'I'm not so backward as I looks.' While her children became more stylized, moon-faced, legless and round-toed, her pictures became more inventive. Unusual perspectives were combined with strong colours and this, with the immediate enclosure of the border, contributed to the overall designs.*

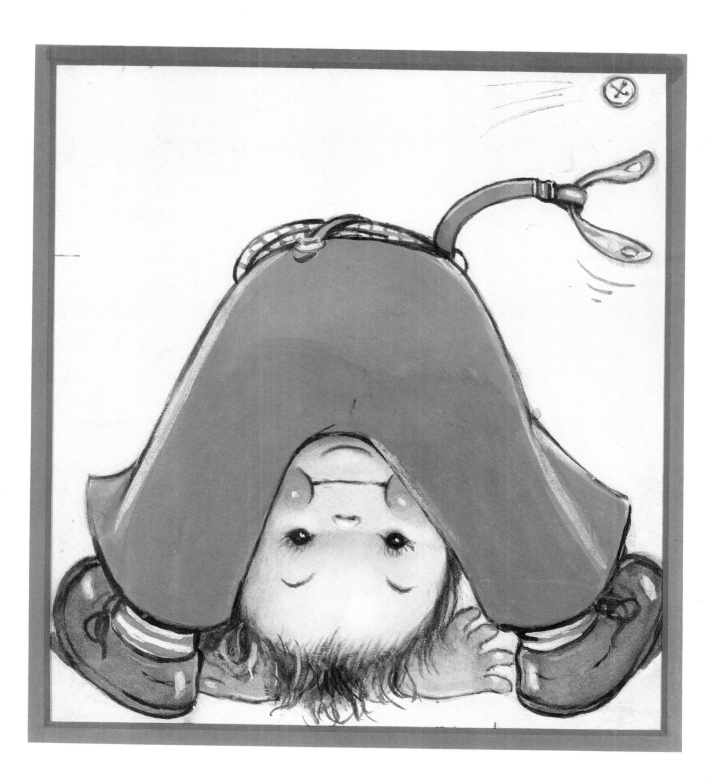

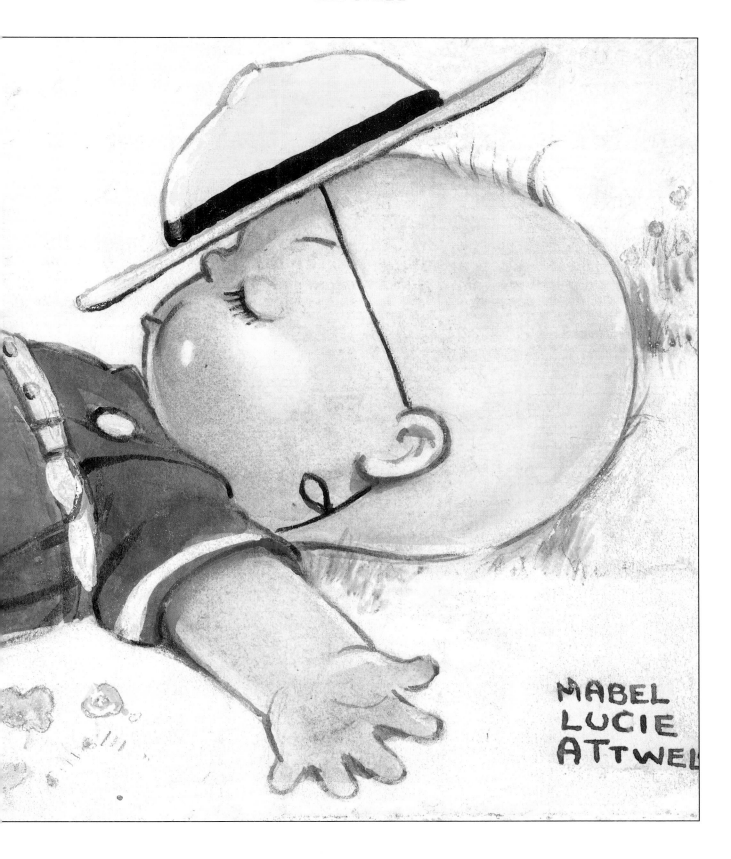

MABEL
LUCIE
ATTWELL

PREVIOUS PAGES 'Laz-y bones – that's me!'
ABOVE 'Forward she went and now she was
attacked by mysterious foes.'
OPPOSITE 'The Fairies came back in numbers and
gambolled as merrily as before.' Both pictures are
from Lucie Attwell's Fairy Book, 1932. Begun in
the early 1900s, her book illustrations only
changed very slightly in style and content. Note
the fairies, last seen in the sky over the Neverland.

'Before we close our blackouts,
This is what we'll do,
You send a loving thought to me,
An' I'll send one to you!'

OPPOSITE 'Careless talk may give away vital
secrets.' Again, in the Second World War, Mabel
Lucie's postcards made their own contribution
though they were not to become as famous as the
Fougasse series, 'Walls have ears'. But they
became popular postcards in these austere times.

OPPOSITE 'Held Up.' From Lucie Attwell's Annual
*of 1933. This artwork recalls the happiest days in
the late 1920s. Mabel Lucie and her husband
bought their first car and the whole family had
many outings to the country.*
*PREVIOUS PAGES The driver in the
postcard is inspired by her husband, Pat – dapper,
bow-tied and with the ever-present cigarette.*

XPECTS ——!

PREVIOUS PAGES
The call to arms is patriotically heeded by Mabel
Lucie's infant body-builder.
OPPOSITE *'Hold it! You're just swell!' The subject*
matter of the postcards stayed fresh and topical to
the end. Part of their popular appeal resulted from
their responsiveness to changes in fad and
fashion.

BIBLIOGRAPHY

That Little Limb by May Baldwir
W. & R. CHAMBERS, 1905 (4 colour
illustrations)

The Amateur Cook by K. Burrill
& Anne M. Booth W. & R.
CHAMBERS, 1905

Troublesome Ursula by Mabel
Quiller-Couch
W. & R. CHAMBERS, 1905 (8 colour
illustrations)

Dora, A High School Girl by May
Baldwin W. & R. CHAMBERS, 1906

The Little Tin Soldier by Graham
Mar W. & R. CHAMBERS, 1909 (6
colour illustrations)

The February Boys by Mrs
Molesworth W. & R. CHAMBERS,
1909 (8 colour illustrations)

Old Rhymes RAPHAEL TUCK AND
SONS, 1909

The Old Pincushion by Mrs
Molesworth W. & R. CHAMBERS,
1910 (8 colour illustrations)

A Band of Mirth by L. T. ('Lillie'
Thomasina) Meade W. & R.
CHAMBERS

That Troublesome Dog by R.
Jacberns W. & R. CHAMBERS

Grimm's Fairy Tales CASSELL &
COMPANY, 1910 (4 colour
illustrations)

Fairy Tales, Stories and Legends
CASSELL & COMPANY, 1910
(4 colour illustrations)

Mother Goose RAPHAEL TUCK
AND SONS, 1910 (12 colour
illustrations)

Alice in Wonderland by Lewis
Carroll RAPHAEL TUCK AND
SONS, 1911 (12 colour
illustrations)

Grimm's Fairy Stories RAPHAEL
TUCK AND SONS (5 colour
illustrations)

*Troublesome Topsy and her
Friends* by May Baldwin W. & R.
CHAMBERS, 1913 (6 colour
illustrations)

Our Playtime Picture Book
RAPHAEL TUCK AND SONS, 1913

Hans Andersen's Fairy Tales
edited by Edric Vredenburg
RAPHAEL TUCK AND SONS, 1914
(12 illustrations)

The Water Babies by Charles
Kingsley (Abridgement)
RAPHAEL TUCK AND SONS, 1915
(12 colour illustrations)

*Children's Stories from French
Fairy Tales* by Doris Ashley
RAPHAEL TUCK AND SONS, 1917

Peeping Pansy by Marie, Queen
of Roumania HODDER AND
STOUGHTON, 1919 (8 illustrations)

Wooden by Archibald Marshall
COLLINS, 1920 (4 illustrations)

*Puss in Boots and other Fairy
Tales* THOMAS NELSON AND
SONS, 1920

Fairyland THOMAS NELSON AND
SONS, 1918 (8 colour illustrations)

Youngest Reader's Fairy Tales
THOMAS NELSON AND SONS
(4 colour illustrations)

*Peggy – The Lucie Attwell Cut-
Out Dressing Doll* VALENTINE &
SONS, 1921

Peter Pan and Wendy by J. M.
Barrie HODDER AND STOUGHTON,
1921 (12 colour illustrations)

*Bunty and the Boo-Boos
The Boo-Boos and Bunty's Baby
The Boo-Boos at School
The Boo-Boos at the Seaside
The Boo-Boos at Honeysweet
Farm
The Boo-Boos and Santa Claus*
VALENTINE & SONS, 1920—22

Baby's Book RAPHAEL TUCK AND
SONS, 1922 (14 colour
illustrations)

*Stitch Stitch – The MLA
Needlework Book of Silks,
Patterns and Weldon's Transfers*
(With needles and silk)
VALENTINE & SONS, 1922

Comforting Thoughts by M. L.
Attwell VALENTINE & SONS

For Today VALENTINE & SONS,
'Golden Thoughts' booklet
(11 colour illustrations)

The Lucie Attwell Annual S.W.
PARTRIDGE & CO., 1922—1926 (This
publication then changed title to
become *Lucie Attwell's
Children's Book*, 1927—1932. Dean
and Son took over publication
and returned the title to *Lucie
Attwell's Annual*, 1933—1974)

Lucie Attwell's Bedtime Stories
S.W. PARTRIDGE & CO., 1923

*Lucie Attwell's Merry Time
Stories* S.W. PARTRIDGE & CO.,
1923

Lucie Attwell's Tea Time Stories
S.W. PARTRIDGE & CO., 1923

*Mother Goose – Nursery Rhymes
for Baby* S.W. PARTRIDGE & CO.

Lucie Attwell's Tales for Bedtime
S.W. PARTRIDGE & CO.

Lucie Attwell's Tales for Teatime
S.W. PARTRIDGE & CO., 1924

*Lucie Attwell's Tales for All
Times* S.W. PARTRIDGE & CO., 1924

The Lucie Attwell Picture Books
S.W. PARTRIDGE & CO., 1924–1928

The Lost Princess, A Fairy Tale
by Marie, Queen of Roumania
S.W. PARTRIDGE & CO., 1924

Lucie Attwell's Twilight Tales by
M. L. Attwell and A. G.
Herbertson S.W. PARTRIDGE &
CO., 1925

Lucie Attwell's Firelight Tales
S.W. PARTRIDGE & CO., 1925

*Lucie Attwell's Going to Bed
Tales* S.W. PARTRIDGE & CO., 1925

Lucie Attwell's Bedtime Tales
S.W. PARTRIDGE & CO., 1926

Lucie Attwell's Merry Time Tales
S.W. PARTRIDGE & CO., 1926

Lucie Attwell's Tea Time Tales
S.W. PARTRIDGE & CO., 1926

*Lucie Attwell's Wide Awake
Tales* S.W. PARTRIDGE & CO., 1927

*Lucie Attwell's Cuddle Time
Tales* S.W. PARTRIDGE & CO., 1927

*Lucie Attwell's Kiddie Winks'
Tales* S.W. PARTRIDGE & CO.,
1927

Lucie Attwell's Tuck Away Tales
S.W. PARTRIDGE & CO., 1928

*Allerlei Von 'Fido' (All About
Fido)* Vienna Wolf (6 colour
illustrations)

Young Peggy in Toyland by
Archibald Marshall COLLINS,
1928

The Golden Goose RAPHAEL
TUCK AND SONS, 1929

Thumbelina and Other Stories by
Hans Christian Andersen
*The Little Brother and Sister and
Other Stories* by The Brothers
Grimm
The Tinder Box
Little Red Riding Hood, 1929
RAPHAEL TUCK AND SONS, 1920
(All with gramophone records)

Peter Pan and Wendy retold by
Mary Byron 2 vols HODDER AND
STOUGHTON, 1929

Lucie Attwell's Cheerie Tales S.W.
PARTRIDGE & CO., 1929

Lucie Attwell's Chick-a-bid Tales
S.W. PARTRIDGE & CO., 1929

Lucie Attwell's Cutie Tales S.W.
PARTRIDGE & CO., 1929

The Red Shoes and Other Stories
by Hans Christian Andersen
RAPHAEL TUCK AND SONS, 1930

The Wild Swans by Hans
Christian Andersen RAPHAEL
TUCK AND SONS (2 colour
illustrations)

Lucie Attwell's Rainy Day Tales
(various authors) S.W.
PARTRIDGE & CO., 1931

On the Way to Fairyland by
Grace Floyd RAPHAEL TUCK AND
SONS

Lucie Attwell's Rock-Away Tales
(various authors) S.W.
PARTRIDGE & CO., 1930

*The Little Shepherdess by Hans
Christian Andersen* RAPHAEL
TUCK AND SONS, 1932

Lucie Attwell's Fairy Book S.W.
PARTRIDGE & CO., 1932

Lucie Attwell's Happy Day Tales
S.W. PARTRIDGE & CO., 1932

Lucie Attwell's Quiet Time Tales
S.W. PARTRIDGE & CO., 1932

Lucie Attwell's Twilight Tales
S.W. PARTRIDGE & CO., 1932

Lucie Attwell's Painting Books
DEAN & SON, 1934

*Lucie Attwell's Great Big Midget
Book* DEAN & SON, 1932

*Lucie Attwell's Great Big Midget
Book* (different version) DEAN
AND SON, 1935

Playtime Pictures CARLTON
PUBLISHING CO., 1935

Lucie Attwell's Story Book DEAN
& SON, 1943

Lucie Attwell's Story Book
(different version) DEAN & SON,
1945

Lucie Attwell's Jolly Book DEAN
& SON, 1953

Lucy Attwell's Story Book
(different version) DEAN & SON,
1953

Lucie Attwell's Pop-up Book
DEAN & SON, 1956

*Lucie Attwell's Nursery Rhymes
Pop-up Book* DEAN & SON, 1958

Lucie Attwell's Storytime Tales
DEAN & SON, 1959

Lucie Attwell's ABC Pop-up Book
DEAN & SON, 1960

Lucie Attwell's Book of Verse
DEAN & SON, 1960

Lucie Attwell's 'Happy Times'
Pop-up Book DEAN & SON, 1961

Lucie Attwell's Book of Rhymes
DEAN & SON, 1962

Lucie Attwell's Humpty Dumpty
Rhymes Pop-up Book DEAN &
SON, 1963

Lucie Attwell's Painting Book No.
2 DEAN & SON, 1963

Lucy Attwell's 'A Little Bird Told
Me!' DEAN & SON, 1964

Lucie Attwell's Stories for Every
Day (various authors) DEAN &
SON, 1964

ILLUSTRATED
CATALOGUES

1980
Brighton Museum Centenary
Exhibition

1984
Chris Beetles Ltd, St James's,
London. Mabel Lucie Attwell
Exhibition

ANNUALS, GIFT BOOKS
AND CHARITY BOOKS

Father Tuck's Annual (edited by
Eric Vredenburg) RAPHAEL
TUCK AND SONS
1905

'The Victory' by M. L. A.
pp.10–11
'Little Bo-Peep' by M.L.A.
pp.44–45
'The Cuddle Place' by M.L.A.
pp.76–77
'Poor Mary Jane' by M.L.A.
pp.102–103

1906
'Which Way Please?' by M.
Attwell p.7
'A Naughty Pair' by M. Attwell
p. 21
'A Goblin Song' by M. Attwell
p.32
'Annetta's Mandoline' by
Margery Williams pp.88–93
'A Sad Tale' by M. L. Attwell
pp.120–121

1907
Title Page
'Long Ago' by M. L. Attwell
pp.26–27
'Dolly' by Edith Prince Snowden
pp.102–103
'Old Friends are Best' by C. Clare
Meyer pp.120–121
'Two Little Snow White Lambs'
by Githa Sowerby pp.163–170
'A Tale of Bad Belinda' by M. L.
Attwell pp.178–181
'What the Moon Saw' by
Constance M. Lowe pp.225–228
1908
Title Pages x 2
'The Squirrel and the Earl's
Daughter' pp.53–61
'The Four Black Brothers of
Innirshee' pp.148–154

1909
Title Pages x 4
'The Old and the New' by Eric
Vredenburg pp.5–6
'The Piccaninnies Bedtime'
words by Constance M. Lowe,
music by C. Egerton Lowe
pp.17–22
'Goodbye!' p.256

1910
Front Cover
Title Page

'An Angel in the House' by Eric
Vredenburg pp.9–16
'Me Wants the Moon' Opp. p.96
'Lullaby Baby' Opp. p.176

1911
Front Cover
'Cherry Stones' by Eric
Vredenburg pp.90–97

1912
Front cover
Title Pages x 3
'The First Favourite' by Eric
Vredenburg pp.5–6
'The Shelf in the Cupboard' by
Eric Vredenburg pp.7–13
'Doggie at the Sea' by M. L.
Attwell pp.64–65
'The Wonderful Bubble' by Eric
Vredenburg p.146–153
'The Dunce' by M.L.A.
pp.208–209

1913
Front Cover
'The Little Dutch Doll' by Eric
Vredenburg pp.135–141
'The Witch' by C.B. p.149

1914
Front Cover

1917
'The Dragon who guarded
nothing' by Mary Heward
pp.137–142

1920
'Taking Home the Geese' Opp.
p.68

Father Tuck's Golden Gift Series
(edited by Eric Vredenburg)
RAPHAEL TUCK AND SONS

'For Somebody's Darling'
'The Man in the Moon' by M. L.
Attwell p.51
'Good Day! We hope to meet you
again soon' p.72

Little Folks
CASSELL & COMPANY
1910
Vol.71 'All on a Fine March
  Morning!' by D. A.
  Courtney p.293

PERIODICALS

Strand Magazine GEORGE
NEWNES

Feb 1917
Vol.53 'The Attwell Children and
Their Creator' Anon.
pp.203–207

Dec 1921
Vol.62 'What a Dream' by M.L.A.
pp.496–497

Dec 1936
Vol.92 'Naughty and Nice by
Austin Moore pp.178–184

Pearson's Magazine C. ARTHUR
PEARSON
Jan 1906
Vol.21 'The Fate of Mr Miser' by
H. Alexander pp.91–95

Apr 1906
'Bonty's Mighty Mouse' by H.
Alexander pp.446–450

May 1906
'The Man in the Moon' by H.
Alexander pp.508–513

Jun 1906
'King Brown I' by H. Alexander
pp.621–623

Oct 1906
Vol.22 'The Voyage of Lyah' by
H. Alexander pp.398–402

Dec 1906
'The Last of the Witches and a
good thing too' by H. Alexander
p.648–654

Nov 1908
Vol.26 'The Gardening Angel' by
A. L. Harris pp.519–522

Aug 1910
Vol.30 'In Slumland by Ada
Leonara Harris pp.202

Jan 1911
Vol.31 'The Prize Competition –
The Tale of an Absent-
minded Father' Anon.
pp.104–105

Sept 1913
Vol.36 'The Star Child' by Ethel
Train pp.244–253

Oct 1915
Vol.40 'The Conversion of the
Twins' by Hilda
Trevelyan Thomson
pp.401–406

Nov 1915
'The Telegram' by Hilda
Trevelyan Thomson pp.487–491

Dec 1915
'Kitchener Clutterbuck' by Hilda
Trevelyan Thomson pp.678–685

Sept 1916
Vol.42 'The Red Cross Nurse' by
Ethel Talbot p.520

Jan 1917
Vol.43 'Daddy's Birthday
Present' by Hilda
Trevelyan Thomson
pp.53–59

May 1919
Vol.47 'The Little Girl who loved
her bed' by Ellaline
Terriss p.385

ACKNOWLEDGEMENTS

A biography is more enjoyable to write from family reminiscences. Mabel Lucie Attwell's son Peter has been unfailingly helpful and given us many first-hand insights. Peggy, her daughter, died a few years ago and it is from her notes that much of the factual information has been obtained. Her children, the Wickham families, have generously given access to all the available papers and original artwork. To them all, especial thanks. Collectors, who like to remain anonymous, still deserve special credit for loan of their originals, and thanks to John Henty for a selection of his ephemera collection. The first comprehensive bibliography is entirely the work of my assistant Debbie Baker. She has done much of the research, the hard work, and this book is shared with her.

The line illustrations in the Bibliography come from Lucie Attwell's Children's Book, *1932, (p.116),* Lucie Attwell's Annual, *1935, (p.117) and* Lucie Attwell's Fairy Book, *1932, (p.118 and p.119).*